Only Jesus

Poems from a Pilgrim Heart

*"Let us go forth therefore unto Him
without the camp, bearing His reproach.
For here have we no continuing city,
but we seek one to come."*
Hebrews 13:13-14

Copyright © 2017 Emily Potter.
Permission granted to copy and distribute
individual poems for personal use.
ISBN: 978-0-9961932-1-4

Photo credits:
Page 44 courtesy of Timothy Potter.
Pages 121 and 167 courtesy of Hannah Potter.
Cover photo courtesy of Timothy Potter.
All other photographs by Emily Potter.
S.D.G.

All Scripture quotations taken from the King
James Version of the Bible.

Table of Contents

Foreword 9
Only Jesus 13
The High Road 14
Hidden Keys 18
Everlasting Arms 23
Above All Keeping. 24
O Thou Who wast Tempted. 30
Be Patient. 35
A Mirror 39
Athirst 43
Nothing More 45
All!. 46
The Fruit of the Spirit 49
Forgive Me, O Lord. 54
A Life of Surrender 59
Constant Forgiveness. 64
To Know as I am Known. 68
In the Darkness 75
Require Much 76
Oh, Father, Why? 81
Peace 87

The Hope of Glory	91
The Well of Joy	94
Promises	98
Keep Me, Lord	105
To Live Each Day	107
Speak but the Word	111
Walk in the Light	115
A Lost Will	119
Tonight	122
Himself	126
Sand by the Sea	129
How Can I Help but Praise Him?	134
Where Your Treasure Is	141
One Golden Spoon	144
Today	149
Sunbeams	153
Stay Still	154
And Yet—	159
My Prayer	163
About the Author	166

Foreword

This book is a candle I would rather have hidden under a bushel. When the Lord first asked me to publish it, I was quite willing. I'd been praying about what to do with the poems He'd given me—more than thirty in just a few months, after perhaps four or five in the last decade—and this was His answer. I started looking into formatting and print costs with the unique excitement of following the Lord's leading.

But then I started thinking. Those poems were something so special, just between the Lord and me—gifts from Him to treasure in secret and share as He led with a few close friends. I shrank from the thought of the world seeing them. Publishing would taint them, commercialize them. Worst of all, I might read them myself through the dreaded lens of what-other-people-will-think rather than purely as they came from the Lord. The more I thought about publishing the book, the less I liked it. That evening I took it back to the Lord.

"Think of all the poems you've read," He said, reminding me of Fanny Crosby, Frances Havergal, Amy Carmichael, and poems that lifted my heart to Him with their ideal of selfless holiness. "Were they spoiled by being published?"

No, of course not. They shone with a heavenly beauty all their own.

"And would you have ever read them if they hadn't been published?"

No. Oh, my Lord knows! Of course He was right. The poems were His, and what joy to think He might make them to others what the poems of those who'd gone before had been to me! The candle's light wasn't mine to hide. And so here is this book.

Each poem has a story. Some grew out of joy, some out of darkness. One came to hold me firm through temptation fiercer than I'd imagined, another to shame my boredom in Numbers' repetitions with glorious lessons from one tiny phrase. Some were written all at once, words flowing freely as the Lord led; others took days of prayer and rewriting. Often I thought there were no poems left to write, but then the Lord would bring another lesson, another verse to mind.

In some ways this book holds the last ten years of my life. They weren't always easy years, but they were beautiful. Ten years ago I gave my Lord everything, and He began giving me Himself in return. I love the thought that the lessons He taught me won't be wasted, or the beauties of His truth lost—He's put them in these poems for me, and now for others.

I once read of a missionary author who laid down her pen on a finished manuscript as words from the book of John came to her mind: "But the servants which drew the water knew." Oh, I knew exactly what she meant! Others might think that she wrote those books—or that I wrote these poems—but she knew the source. Those who draw from the Master's supply know that anything of power or value comes only from Him.

"The servants which drew the water knew." May the servant be out of sight, and the Master fill all in all.

Emily Potter
Fruitvale, Idaho
April, 2017

Only Jesus

He can satisfy my heart,
Fill each lonely, longing part
With His Spirit's gentle art;
Only Jesus.

To my weary, sin-sick soul,
He's the serpent on the pole—
Just one look and I am whole.
Only Jesus.

When I'm anxious, harried, pressed,
Just one moment on His breast,
Eyes on Him, and all is rest;
Only Jesus.

Mercies fresh with each new day,
Never grudging, never gray,
Though I oh, so often stray—
Only Jesus.

Oh, my Lord, what can I do?
I am nothing but for You;
Let me follow, meek and true,
Only Jesus.

The High Road

Oh, lead me on the High Road, Lord,
Through all my earthly race;
Eyes glancing not to left or right,
But straight into Your face.

The High Road rises straight and sure,
Each step on solid truth;
On either side the coaxing world
Wields flashing lures of youth.

One step from off the High Road,
With an aim to pleasing man,
And my feet sink in the broad morass
Of trackless, shifting sand.

Then, oh—where is the High Road?
From the swamp I cannot see;
Confusion fills my soul, hope shrinks;
Thick darkness covers me.

A voice from off the High Road—
Still and small, oh, vastly dear!
Calls my heart, and I remember:
He has promised—He is here.

The way back to the High Road
Is a look, a prayer, a cry;
And my Lord, e'er ready, waiting,
Sets me firmly by His side.

He will keep me on the High Road,
Though I wander oft and far;
His the strength, the tender mercy;
His dear face my guiding star.

To His homeland leads the High Road;
March straight on, the battle's won!
When my climbing days are over,
This my welcome—His "well done."

Hidden Keys

No glory in this world, Lord, may I seek,
Except the glorious joy of knowing Thee;
In all afflictions quiet, calm, and meek,
For hidden in each trial is a key.

A key to change my heart to match Thine own;
A key unlocking knowledge of Thy ways;
A key to turn each trouble into joy;
If I but find it, richly it repays.

For irritation's key unlocks the door
To patience that no other school can teach;
Unpleasant tasks hold keys to unlock joy;
The door to cheerful service is in reach.

Forbearance hides its key in stinging words,
Forgiveness' door is only found through hurt;
Temptation yields the key to self-control;
Pure jewels are often buried deep in dirt.

Through long-drawn hardship
    perseverance grows;
A meek heart comes through overbearing
    strife;
In days of pain compassion's key lies hid;
In death, the key to hope of endless life.

Cruel disappointment's key to gratitude
Gives thanks for all plans formed for
    good above;
In loneliness a precious key of grace
Unlocks my Savior's all-sufficient love.

Oh, let me search and seek until I find
The reason for each trial—each hidden
    key;
For every tribulation, grief, or loss,
Swings wide a door that leads me close to
    Thee.

Everlasting Arms

My heart, fear thou no loss, no change,
No numbing grief, no quick alarm;
For underneath thy frailty,
His strength—the everlasting arms.

In irritations, grating, small,
In pain from friend-inflicted harm,
In Him find refuge, calm, secure—
The peace of everlasting arms.

When hopes grow faint and tarry long,
When tarnished dreams have lost their
    charm,
Renew thy vision—glory waits!
Trust on in everlasting arms.

In restless suff'ring, quiet joy
To trace, my heart, His kindness warm;
And e'en in death, sink back—He'll bear
Thee home in everlasting arms.

Above All Keeping

"Keep thy heart above all keeping, for out of it are the issues of life." Proverbs 4:23, margin

Above all keeping, keep your heart,
Warns wisdom's wisest voice;
From it the springs of life all flow,
Each word, each thought, each choice.

How keep my heart? I've tried and failed
To watch, and guard, and guide;
It turns, deceives, and slips away,
Enmeshed in sin and pride.

O Lord, I give my heart to You;
'Tis Yours—oh, hold it fast;
Keep living waters springing pure,
Untouched by earth's gray blast.

Keep all my heart for You, my Lord,
And all affections guard;
Oh, let me love as one with You,
When loving seems too hard.

Oh, guard my heart with words of truth,
Whose entrance giveth light;
And fill it with thanksgiving's song
In darkest days of night;

Well-stocked with treasures old and new
From scripture's rich-veined mines,
For You to bring forth as You will,
In golden, singing lines.

Oh, keep it stayed on promises
Of daily strength and grace,
Of sin submerged, forgotten, purged;
Of light to run my race.

I beg for it Your Spirit's pow'r,
To comfort, cleanse, uplift;
More willing, Lord, than parents dear,
Are You to give that gift.

Oh, guard it from impurity,
In word, in thought, in act;
Let holiness its watchword be,
Your blood its solemn pact.

"Above all keeping, keep your heart;"
My Lord is keeping mine,
And I in trust keep watch with Him,
Till heaven's beauties shine.

O Thou Who wast Tempted

Earth's desires are dragging my soul like the tide;
I'm fighting, but slipping—the pit's mouth looms wide;
Oh, Thou who wast tempted in all things as I,
Help me, help me now.

"Resist ye the devil, and then he will flee;
Then crucify lust, yield your members to Me."
Oh, Savior, I will! Oh, Lord God, hear my plea!
Show me, show me how.

More than all they that watch for the morning, wait I;
As a dove to its window, for refuge I fly;
From the depths of my sin to my Savior I cry,
Hide me, hide me now.

In His hand I will hide, till the storm is
    o'erpast;
By His side in white linen stand blameless
    at last;
At His feet, rapt in glory, my life's crown
    to cast,
Let me, let me bow.

Be Patient

Be patient therefore, brethren, till the
    coming of the Lord;
We count the prophets happy who
    endured and kept His word;
Stand firm upon His promise, set your
    hearts upon His name;
Be patient till He calls you; those who
    wait will know no shame.

Be patient when the light is low, and
    keep your lamps trimmed bright;
Work quickly now before the gloom
    descends and all is night.
Be patient for the harvest; sow good seed
    in God's employ;
Tears now will be forgotten reaping
    promised sheaves of joy.

Be patient, soldier on, stand fast, as
    seeing One unseen;
In suff'ring uncomplaining, whether
    days are full or lean;

For one day all will be put right; this
   moment's grief erased;
Be patient therefore, brethren—at the door
   your Savior waits.

A Mirror

Oh, Lord, from You
Comes all I have
Of grace of tongue or pen;
From You all love,
All loveliness;
All pow'r to hearten men.

And as from You
All good gifts flow,
All thanks and praise return;
Oh, let me not
For one small jot
Of Your due glory yearn.

Let my weak life
A mirror be,
Reflecting only You;
E'er pointing men
To Christ, with my
Poor figure of the True.

Oh, fill me, Lord—
Your word invites;

My mouth is open wide.
Your Spirit pour
Through my life's door
To all the world outside.

Athirst

Athirst for holiness in mind and heart,
I find no cup that fills me but Thine
    own;
Oh, Living Water, satisfy me now,
And let me drink forever at Thy throne.

Oh, Bread of heaven, soul-fulfilling
    Word,
I crave Thee more than necessary food;
Oh, turn my hungry heart from famine's
    gloom
To feast upon the fullness of my Lord.

The one who comes to Thee shall never
    hunger,
And he who trusts Thy word shall never
    thirst;
Oh, keep me coming, trusting Thee
    forever,
Filled every moment fully as at first.

Nothing More

My heart has the love of the King of kings;
He chose me for His bride;
How can I long for anything more?
Why does my heart turn aside?

My bridegroom designed me to please
 Himself;
My Lord makes no mistakes;
Why do I wish for what He hasn't given,
Indulging my heart when it aches?

My Lord always gives me whatever is best;
No good will He hold back;
As soon as it's good for me, lo—it will
 come!
Why pine as if something I lack?

When my eyes are on Christ, then my soul
 is all joy,
All intense satisfaction and peace;
Nothing more on this earth do I need—do
 I want—
Only Christ; all to Him I release.

All!

"Cast all your cares on Him"—our Lord—
"Because He cares for you."
But all my cares—do You mean *all?*
My Savior, *all* on You?

You care for every little thing?
His word unflinching calls—
And all means all; that small word πας:
Each, any, every, *all*.

Then oh, my Lord, how smooth my life
And all my days should be!
If all my cares are cast on You,
There's nothing left for me!

The Fruit of the Spirit

On the tree of my life,
Oh, my Lord, do I see
The fruit of the Spirit
Growing in me?

Do I see, Lord, Your love,
Serving, caring, and kind,
Putting others' needs first,
Lifting burdens that grind?

And Your joy, Lord, that rests
Underneath all my days,
Do I see its glad fruit,
And rejoice in Your ways?

Do I see now Your peace,
Passing all human ken,
Ruling, keeping my heart,
Loving laws from Your pen?

And longsuffering's fruit,
Patient strength to endure,
Quiet trust in Your plans—
Is its fruit springing pure?

Is Your gentleness—calm,
Not retorting in kind,
Answ'ring softly in strife—
Setting fruit on my vine?

And Your goodness, that leads me
To shining-eyed praise,
Is it bearing its righteous,
Pure fruit in my days?

Is the fruit of my faith,
Planted firm in Your word,
Bearing deeds done in You,
Living truth that I've heard?

And is meekness—acceptance
Of Your work and will,
Submission in trial—
Is it growing still?

My branch made for temperance,
Full self-control,
Will its buds ever blossom
With fruit from my soul?

When I look to myself, Lord,
For fruit on my tree,
I joy in Your work,
But I mourn, Lord, for me;

For my flesh is so broken,
So weak and so flawed,
That it never could blossom
Pure fruit for my God.

But then, Lord, I lift up
My eyes to Your grace;
Not my flesh, but Your Spirit
Yields fruit in my place.

Oh, let me but seek
Your pure Spirit's rich flow,
And without my poor worries,
Your own fruit will grow.

Forgive Me, O Lord

Forgive me, O Lord, for accepting Your gifts,
So many, so rich and so free,
But forgetting the One who so endlessly gives,
While my heart is distracted with me.

Oh, Lord, let me look single-hearted to You,
All needs, all successes aside;
Only loving, adoring, and lost in Your praise,
While all else fades to nothing beside.

Let my worship be daily submission to You,
All my self on the altar of life,
Holding nothing my own, living but as You lead,
Self forgotten in soul-winning strife.

Oh, my Savior, my King, when in Your grace alone,

I have done some small work for Your
 name,
Then guard me from giving one thought
 to myself;
Let my heart seek Your face just the same.

A channel, a vessel, all empty and clean,
Only waiting Your Spirit's full flow,
Something clear and invisible, Lord,
 would I be,
Only living Your beauty to show.

Then I'll praise You, O Lord, for Your
 gifts, full and free;
All my springs, life, and love—all in You;
And forgetting myself, set my face up
 toward heav'n,
Christ my song, till life's singing is
 through.

A Life of Surrender

Living a life of surrender
To the matchless Creator of all,
Who knows all of my ends from
    beginnings,
And moves endless worlds with His call;
Who plans out every day, every moment,
In the working of marvelous love,
Is no folly, but highest adventure,
Truest wisdom, full pow'r from above.

It will cost me my life to surrender;
My decisions, affections, and will;
Yea, my innermost self must go under;
No desire of my own may I fill.
No more freedom to choose my direction;
Every step at Another's command;
Every thought must be held for inspection;
Every movement made under His hand.

Is it worth it, my Lord, to surrender?
How count worth in such glorious terms!
How name joy swelling upward inside me
Till it threatens to burst all its berms!

Oh, the fountain of exhilaration
Of one day spent in step with my King;
And the thrill of advancing a purpose
That to glimpse sends my heart on its wing!

Is it worth it to give up myself, Lord?
Who would not change their dust for pure gold!
Fling away all earth's self-loving shadows,
As the glories of heaven unfold.
Leave unrest for the peace passing knowledge,
Stumbling steps for the sure tread of hope;
Failing eyes catch the vision of glory;
Fumbling hands grasp a firm-anchored rope.

Is it worth it? My heart shouts the answer,
Though, forgetting, it twinges and fails;
For so quickly my self clings to earth-loves,
With such grip that my poor courage quails.
Is it worth it? One look at my Savior,

And my tears turn from pain to His
    peace;
He knows, oh, He *knows*, and He loves
    me;
At His feet all my murmurings cease.

There is pow'r in a life of surrender,
Pow'r to follow our great Risen King;
There is joy, sheer excitement and
    pleasure,
Tending fruit for eternity's spring.
There is pain, daily dying, and anguish,
As our self fights each gasp to the last;
But the prize of a life of surrender
Is a life where surrender is past.

When surrender is past—oh, what glory!
To be one with our Savior and Friend;
Self and sin no more even remembered;
Immortality's joys know no end.
So my life, Lord, to Thee I surrender,
No reserve, no retreat, no regret;
Send Your grace when the battle is
    fiercest,
Till surrender with triumph is met.

Constant Forgiveness

Constant forgiveness,
My Lord gives to me;
Constant forgiveness,
Ungrudging and free.

Constant forgiveness,
When crying I pray,
"It just isn't fair
To forgive me today;

"That's the hundredth time
That I've done the same thing;
I can't ask again
For forgiveness, my King."

Then my Lord softly answered,
"It's not based on you;
It's not for your sake
I forgive as I do.

"It's never been you;
I forgive for my Son;

I only see Christ,
And forgiveness is won."

Oh, what freedom, what joy!
My debt already paid!
My forgiveness is there,
The exchange long since made.

I am hiding in Christ;
When my Lord looks at me,
He sees His dear Son,
And His cross sets me free.

Constant forgiveness!
Oh, Lord, when I fall,
Let me run straight to You—
Christ has finished it all!

To Know as I am Known

That I may know as I am known—
Oh, glimpse of vision fair!
To fully know my Savior's worth,
His beauty, love, and care.

To know His depths of kindness,
His wells of princely peace;
His pow'r that formed each living cell,
And made the storm surge cease.

To know His perfect wisdom,
Unmatched and unexcelled;
To know the all-sufficient Hand
In which my heart is held.

To know His full submission,
To glimpse His glory's cost:
The Name on high above all names
Was christened on the cross.

To know His measured judgment,
Where truth and mercy blend;
Where righteous peace is on the throne,
And all injustice ends.

To know His gracious fullness,
His all-supplying vine;
The root that fills all unmet needs
Is grafted into mine.

To know Him as He is, and then
Be like Him—oh, what bliss!
Not futile hope, but certainty—
All heaven's joy is this!

To know Him is eternal life,
And yet He gives me more—
The love the Father shares with Him
They both upon me pour.

To know that love—that cannot be!
For me, an earthly clod?
But Christ has prayed, and promised it—
The full, rich love of God.

To know as I am known—someday
The darkling glass will break;
Earth's dust will drop asleep, and in
His undimmed image wake.

That I may know as I am known,
Is all my soul's desire;
Oh, teach me, Lord, through suffering,
To meet Thee in the fire.

In the Darkness

In the darkness of my soul-self,
When I look to me alone,
Oh, the danger of a shipwreck
Facing sea storms on my own!

Or when eyes are turned toward others,
Who, though valiant, fail as I,
I find but a false foundation,
Shifting shoals, and changing tides.

But above my changeful darkness
Shines a Star serene and clear,
Guiding, changeless, till the morning,
When my Savior's face appears.

Require Much

Require much of me, O Lord,
With Thine own strength to give it;
Such boundless wealth you've given me,
Such richness of Thy Spirit.

Require much of sacrifice,
And let me know Thy beauty—
Thy love-driv'n emptying of self,
Thy joy in hardest duty.

Require much of suffering;
I would of Thine partake,
In fellowship naught else can gain;
My thirst for Thee thus slake.

Require much, and keep me, Lord,
In holy trust abiding;
For I, like Thee, would perfect be—
Oh, let me love Thy chiding.

Require much of toil and pain,
But oh! Leave me Thy Spirit;

Take not Thy daily, guiding light,
Till I my crown inherit.

Require much, but let me dwell
With Thee in humble gladness;
Where cherubim Thy praises swell,
My heart forgets all sadness.

Require much, till death, my Lord,
And let me still remember,
E'en Christ prayed thrice for strength
    to die;
Grace blooms in dark December.

Where much is given, much required;
Require much, my King!
Remind me of this prayer, till joys
Eclipse all suffering.

Oh, Father, Why?

Oh, Father, why—
Though hard I try—
Can I not do
My best for You?

My heart is set
On You, and yet
Each day I fail,
And fall, and wail.

My frame is dust,
And moth and rust
Eat all my hay
And straw away;

"Good deeds," but not
In Your way wrought;
By self all stained;
No true fruit gained.

All rags and dirt,
And hearts left hurt—
Can I no true,
No good thing do?

Not I, but Christ!
With Him I tryst
And He my soul
In love makes whole.

In Him I die,
Yet live—that by
His life in me,
All Christ may see.

His light, not mine,
Makes dark hearts shine;
His words, His hand;
His strength, His plan.

His peace, His grace,
In each new place,
To serve and care
For each one there.

My old heart dead,
And in its stead
One full to brim
With naught but Him!

And though each day
I sigh and say,
My flesh still lives—
What grace He gives!

With joy I see
The "why"—that He
In my dark night
Might blaze forth light.

That I all praise
To Him might raise;
For all I do
Of good is You!

Peace

As the peace of a lingering spring twilight,
Poppies nodding their heads in the breeze,
While the alpenglow crimsons the
    mountains,
And the world lies in calm, dusky ease;

As the peace of a summer at sundown,
When the hills are all shadows and gold,
And the cows turn toward home in the
    meadow,
As the beauties of sunset unfold;

As the peace of a lakeside in August,
Great white thunderheads over the pines,
Three wild geese swimming silent and
    stately,
Trailing mirrors of rippling lines;

As the peace of a cool day in autumn,
Every sound by the misty clouds hushed,
When a clean breeze sweeps chill through
    the hayloft—
Quiet lull in the harvestime's rush;

As the peace of a calm winter evening,
Moonlight glist'ning like jewels on the snow,
While the stars twinkling clear in the heavens
Find their echoes in snow-stars below;

As the peace of a whispering snowflake,
Softly swishing a path through the air,
Floating down to a swift, gentle landing
On a drift with its snow-cousins there;

So the peace of my Lord comes down softly,
Bringing pardon and grace to my heart;
Not the peace of a moment that's passing,
But a peace that need never depart.

The Hope of Glory

The hope of glory!
Christ in me,
Mere taste of things to come,
That lights my life with living Love
And builds my heav'nly home.

The hope of glory!
Promise giv'n
By One who cannot lie;
The work begun—it *shall* be done;
His grace all needs supply.

The hope of glory!
In His hand
He holds us till that day,
When, all fulfilled, the flesh is killed—
All earth-stains washed away.

The hope of glory!
Light unknown,
Unearthly, beams afar;
He promised those who overcome
A gift—the morning star.

The hope of glory!
Drawing near—
The dawn of Christ's great day;
Lift up your heads, redemption's Sun
Is rising—rise, we pray!

The hope of glory!
Silent wait
The King of beauty's call,
To leave this lower place of pain
For glory's golden hall.

The hope of glory!
Realized,
All fear shall drop away;
All sin destroyed, immortal joy
Shall fill our souls that day.

The hope of glory!
Hope no more,
But glorious sight shall be;
The Lamb's pure light in heaven bright
Throughout eternity.

The Well of Joy

A well of joy I have,
To draw from day by day;
A well sunk deep in Jesus' love,
A hidden help and stay.

His joy in me, made full,
Abiding, deep, and strong;
Each time I thirst, and draw again,
He fills my heart with song.

One black night, far from home,
Alone, and lonely, too,
Depression came to visit me,
And pain lent its dark hue.

I looked up to my Lord;
If now His hand could cheer,
When all conspired to bleak despair,
No future cloud I'd fear.

"Draw on My joy," He said,
A thought to me all new;

I reached my heart in hope to Him—
Joy's light came flooding through.

That night I found His well;
It's never yet run dry;
Half-doubting, still I find it full,
And shall until I die.

Promises

The God who hung the galaxies
And deep-hid gems designed,
Has stooped to bind almighty strength
With pledges to mankind.

No obligation forced His hand,
No debt to man He owed;
Pure love as sure as stars above
These promises bestowed.

No pow'r in heaven or earth can change
The pledges God has made;
Our faith can rest with fearless zest
In His protecting shade.

The seasons run unfailing round,
The daybreak follows night;
The seedtime leads to harvest
As the sun lends promised light.

We fear no flood o'er earth or soul,
While banding rainbows glow;
Though waters rise, the Lord has pledged
The flood shall not o'erflow.

He's promised grace in times of need,
And strength to meet each day;
He's pledged for His own goodness' sake
To guide the sinner's way.

Stained hearts are blood-washed white as
    snow,
By His own faithfulness;
As we confess, His justice cleanses
All unrighteousness.

Our faith through every trial here
Is turned to burnished gold;
In speechless, blameless, matchless joy
His face we shall behold.

A crown of life, the morning star,
A secret, unknown name;
A place to walk among His saints,
Amidst the stones of flame.

The tree of life at last unbarred—
Twelve heav'nly fruits to taste;
Twelve gates of single, lustrous pearls,
Twelve jeweled foundations placed.

This city where all glory reigns—
My Savior's promised land;
My everlasting home above,
Prepared by His own hand.

Most glorious pledge of all to me—
With Him to dwell as one;
In light, in love, in holiness,
With *Him*, th'eternal sun!

Exceeding great and passing fair,
These precious promised words,
But fairer still the One who pledged
His love to us—our Lord.

All honor, glory, blessing, praise,
While sun and moon shall shine,
Be Yours, great promise-keeping King,
As You in love are mine.

Keep Me, Lord

Oh, keep me, Lord, with my heart and mind
Attuned to Thy Spirit's word,
And bind my soul and my will to Thine
With a golden, deathless cord.

Oh, keep me, Lord, with my eyes on high,
All affection laid above;
With naught in this world but Thyself and I,
And that "I" swallowed up in Thy love.

Oh, keep me, Lord, to Thy pathway true;
Let me suffer in joy with Thee,
Whether daily thorns or a martyr's due—
As the grace, Thine the glory be.

Oh, keep me, Lord, for Thyself alone,
To be given and used at will;
For in those I serve, I serve Thee, my Own;
In Thy heart, Lord, keep me still.

To Live Each Day

To live each day
With Christ as King
In undisputed sway;
My heart and mind
And life to rule,
My self His loving,
Willing tool,
E'en though for Him
I seem a fool—
'Tis joy no words can say.

To hear His voice—
My Shepherd's call—
Direct each step I take,
Lights ev'ry daily
Household chore
With rays of love
From heaven's shore;
'Tis all for *Him*,
Thus joy; and more—
A gift of love I make.

To praise His name
With all my heart—
His glorious holiness;
His perfect grace,
His justice sure,
His mercy true,
His pleasure pure,
His love that through
All time endures—
How dare my soul do less?

Speak but the Word

Speak but the word, O my Lord and my King,
And whatever You say shall be done;
For all power in heaven and earth rests in You,
The all-loving, all-just Three in One.

Speak but the word, and my storm shall be stilled,
Till Your peace reigns supreme in my heart;
But though thunderbolts crash, while midst hailstones I dash,
Let my trust rise as lightnings close dart.

Speak but the word, and my dry bones shall live,
As Your Spirit breathes life to my soul;
Uphold me, restore me, create my heart clean,
Let me sing as Your grace makes me whole.

Speak but the word, and my trials are gone—
But with them, my chance of reward;
For only on earth can I join in Your pain,
And win gold under suffering's sword.

Speak but the word, Lord, and open the eyes
Of those that I love who are blind;
For—oh, how can I bear that their hearts should not share
In Your love, nor salvation's light find?

Speak but the word, and my soul shall be healed—
But those words from the cross Christ has cried!
"It is finished"—full payment, full cleansing and peace;
That bestowed, no good gift is denied.

Speak but the word—You have spoken, my King!
Precious promises naught can destroy;
Let Your free gift of faith and Your pure, living Word
Guide me onward and up toward Your joy.

Walk in the Light

Walk in the light!
O ye soldier of truth,
Every vestige of darkness abhor.
Ever strive to be pure;
Flee each bright, tempting lure;
March on bravely to Heaven's fair shore.

Walk in the light!
Let no sin, fondly held,
Find a place in your blood-redeemed breast.
Ye are no more your own,
And your Lord hath full shown
That to please Him brings grace, peace and rest.

Walk in the light!
Fix your eyes up above;
Have respect to the wealth of reward.
E'er make diligent search
Lest some stain should besmirch
The fair name of your most holy Lord.

Walk in the light!
In a glass we behold
The e'er matchless ideal of our Lord.
Oh, wholeheartedly gaze,
That the Spirit may raise
Us to mirror His glory and Word.

A Lost Will

Oh, Father, have I lost my will?
At times I think it's vanished;
And then the joy that surging grows—
Perhaps at last it's banished!

But then it's back, that stubborn thing,
That whines, and balks, and trembles,
Pretending that it wants Your way,
While deep down it dissembles.

It only wants just what it wants;
I've tried but failed to kill it;
It lurks beneath the surface there,
And bids me—now!—fulfill it.

Oh, Lord, I know Your ways are best;
With all my heart I say it;
But still my will will rise, with shrill
Demands that I obey it.

Oh, Lord, the worlds embrace Your will;
The whirlwinds bow before it;

The proud waves pause at its command;
The cherubim adore it.

The mountains stand, or step aside,
The stars withdraw their shining;
The lightning flicks its fearsome tongue,
Its twisting flame-roots twining.

The roses climb, and bloom, and blush,
At seasons You've appointed;
And He most fully filled Your will
Who by it was anointed.

Oh, let my will in homage join
With Christ and all creation;
Subdued by sovereign power—Your own—
And lost in adoration.

Tonight

Oh, Father God, my Lord, You know
How happy I am in You tonight;
You know my love, my praise to You,
My thanks for kindness beaming bright.

I praise You, Lord, for all Your grace,
For Your dear guiding, leading hand,
For joy upwelling deep within,
For glimpses of Immanuel's land.

For strength to walk with You today,
Through pain and weakness, hard and
    grim,
For shining light of joy tonight,
For Christ, mine always, only Him.

Oh, Lord, I lift my eyes to You,
So full of joy I cannot speak;
In silent peace I worship You,
Whom all my treasure is to seek.

All I desire is You, my King,
With nothing else beside;

No other love in earth or heav'n,
No other place I hide.

I sing within my heart to You,
A glorious, wordless song;
Oh, let me see Your beauty now,
And worship all life long.

Himself

I close the book of my desires,
And lay it on the shelf;
I stretch my lonely hands to Him;
He fills them—with Himself.

Sand by the Sea

Largeness of heart as the sand by the sea
Was Your gift to the king—oh, Lord,
 give it to me!
A heart like Your own, boundless, open,
 and free,
With room for all men, as You found
 room for me.

A heart that the billows can beat but not
 break,
A heart that, untroubled, can give and
 not take.
A heart hiding treasures of You and
 Your word,
A heart that is happy to hear, not be
 heard.

A heart that pain's footprints can softly
 erase,
Letting tides of Your mercy smooth out
 every trace.
A heart that lies warm in Your bright
 summer sun,

And holds lingering rays till the winter is done.

A heart that can ripple with laughter and light,
Or weep with those caught in cold grief-waves at night.
A heart that gives footing to those drifting far,
By pointing them back to the clear Morning Star.

A heart that seeks ever the drowning to save,
With a rope twined by One who has vanquished the grave.
A heart unconcerned with the world's wisest ways;
They wash on, but what stands on the Rock firmly stays.

A heart built of bits of pure glass, crystal clear,
Tumbled under life's waves till Your likeness appears;
Tiny jewels of Your lessons, to flash in Your sun,

Till the dust-life is over, and heaven is
   won.

Largeness of heart as the sand by the sea;
Oh, the beauty that word-picture calls up
   for me!
A heart like Your own—but, in Christ, it
   is mine!
Let my heart, grain by grain, with Your
   boundless love shine.

How Can I Help but Praise Him?

How can I help but praise Him,
My Savior and my King?
For giving His own self for me—
How can I help but sing?

For holding all things in His hand,
The world, my life, my heart;
For gentleness that maketh great,
And humble grace imparts.

For joy unending, boundless, free,
Drawn from salvation's well,
With darkness grasping all around;
That joy no tongue can tell.

For love that takes me by surprise
With gifts just meant for me;
The universe's King prepared
That flower for me to see.

For beauty that enthralls my soul,
In crag, in cloud, in tree;

Each made for His own pleasure—yes,
And freely shared with me.

For giving earthly eyes a sight
No endless gazing mars:
Thy glorious, holy, matchless face,
That naught can stain nor scar.

To gaze unending is to find
A peace no pow'r can shake,
A guidance sure, a pleasure pure,
All for the Savior's sake.

For power that sets the world a-spin
And orders all my days
In love, and for the highest good—
How can I help but praise?

For mercy sure as firmest rock,
To Christ in justice due;
For searing, scouring, cleansing blood
To purge my old heart new.

For hope that nothing can dispel,
Because it rests on Thee;

For faith, a Father's gift of love,
When only pain I see.

For streams of glory here on earth
In fellowship with Thee,
For promise of unsullied joy
Throughout eternity.

For—oh, my God!—Thy glorious Self,
To me in Jesus given,
I'll sing Your praise through all my days,
And joy!—still sing in heaven!

Where Your Treasure Is

"For where your treasure is, your heart
 will be."
Those oft-read words now blaze with
 sudden light,
And show the way to gain my heart's
 desire—
To love my Lord with all my self and
 might.

Why, here, my soul, the secret lies quite
 plain;
To have your whole heart given to the
 Lord,
Just give Him all your treasures, one by
 one;
Your heart will follow; 'tis your Savior's
 word.

And, oh, my Lord, I've seen You prove it
 true;
Each off'ring binds me closer to Your side;
With full surrender fuller love has grown,
Through sacrifice I nearer still abide.

Oh, Lord, each treasure that You bring to mind,
May I lift up with open hands to You;
My time, affections, earthly wealth and dreams,
All I hold dear, and love to see and do.

And then perhaps the treasure greater still,
The one that most displays that longed-for love—
A simple, full obedience may I yield,
Each passing day until I pass above.

For naught on earth can touch the searing joy
Of knecling, lost in wondering love of You;
I gladly sell all else for that one pearl,
All treasure freely giv'n—my heart pursues.

One Golden Spoon

"And it came to pass on the day that Moses had fully set up the tabernacle...that the princes of Israel, heads of the house of their fathers... brought their offering before the LORD... one golden spoon of ten shekels, full of incense."
Numbers 7:1-3, 26

One golden spoon,
Ten shekels weight
Of gold most pure and fine,
The princes brought
In each man's lot,
A gift for God divine.

One golden spoon
I long to be;
Pure gold, by fire refined.
A vessel tried
And sanctified,
Heart, soul, will, strength, and mind.

One golden spoon,
Of incense full,
Each prince to God did bring;

On altar's flame,
To heaven came
Their fragrant offering.

One golden spoon,
Oh, may I be;
E'er full of incense sweet:
The prayers that rise
Before Thine eyes,
As saints kneel at Thy feet.

One golden spoon—
That would I be;
A small but holy thing,
To purely do,
Prayer-filled and true,
The service of the King.

Today

Oh, Lord, today it all went wrong;
You seemed far off,
I lost my song;
Confused, depressed, guilt-torn and tired,
Direction lost,
Soul uninspired.

But every time I came to You,
The fog rolled back,
The light shone through;
I glimpsed the joy of other days,
Then lost myself
Again in haze.

Alone with You, and in Your word,
What gleams of grace,
What peace unheard!
But then outside, distractions round,
The mist swirled up
And dragged me down.

Then late tonight, a song You gave:
Press onward, up,

Unfettered, brave,
To higher ground, above the world—
The clouds slid back,
Your sun unfurled!

Oh, lift me up to live in light—
In crowds, alone,
By day, by night—
Untouched by clamor, stage, or place,
Beholding Your
Unclouded face.

Sunbeams

Heaviness makes a heart to stoop;
A good word makes it glad;
Oh, send me sunbeam words of truth,
To share when hearts are sad.

Stay Still

Stay still, my self, and hush your thoughts
From running without end;
Stand still to hear your Savior's voice,
And to His word attend.

Take time—a minute here, or there—
To pause in heart and mind;
To look above earth's rushing stream
And Christ's calm presence find.

Take time to draw aside with Him,
To feast upon His word;
To fill your soul with light and truth,
At table with your Lord.

A moment to prepare your heart
To seek your Savior's face,
Has changed the course of kingly lives,
For honor or disgrace.

Lord, let me pause and look to You,
For peace when troubles roll;

In multitudes of tumbling thoughts
Your comforts soothe my soul.

Oh, let me as a handmaid wait
The guidance of Your hand;
Nor take a hasty step, but move
As one with Your command.

Take time, stay still; now hush, my heart!
Your flurried worries cease;
A pause to set your mind on Christ
Brings perfect, present peace.

And Yet–

My God who cares for dust and mud—
You know that's all I am.
A failing, foolish, fumbling worm,
And yet—Your close-held lamb.

You know my pride that weed-like sprouts
And clings, and climbs and grows
On all vain nothings in my soul,
And yet—Your love bends low.

You know my mind that wanders far
From truth, to twisted lies;
That hails as hero worthless self,
And yet—Your Word still guides.

You know my heart, that longs for You,
But daily swerves aside
For passing, jangling, fleshly lust,
And yet—Your grace abides.

You know me, Lord; You knew me when
My Savior died for me,

Your sin-bound, twice-dead enemy,
And yet—You set me free.

You know my daily battles, Lord;
You gain my victory.
On earth my old man drags me down,
And yet—I'll rise with Thee!

My Prayer

Oh fill my eyes, my mind, my heart
With all Thy greatness, all Thou art,
With grace and glory, majesty—
Oh let me, Lord, see only Thee.

Let no dark pathos, no bright dream,
No hero's triumph, battle's gleam,
Or world's adventure me enthrall.
Be all, my Savior; all in all.

Oh, let me walk so close to Thee
That I am lost—there is no *me*,
But only Christ, consuming Fire,
And I Thy burning, living pyre.

Let me not long for man's embrace,
But solely, wholly, seek Thy face,
My eyes alight, my heart aflame,
My torch Thy word, my love Thy name.

Oh, fill my eyes, enchain my soul,
Let lust and fear forgotten roll
Beneath Thy Spirit's conqu'ring tide;
Oh, vanquish sin, and self, and pride.

Tear out my bent toward pleasing men,
That subtle shift of voice or pen,
And let me pure, clear-hearted be,
As when, alone, I kneel with Thee.

Oh, hold me close, Lord—carry me;
I have no strength to walk with Thee.
Sin slain, I'll see Thy face one day;
Till then—oh, fill my eyes, I pray.

About the Author

I wasn't planning to put this part in. I'd rather have stayed under the bushel myself, but the Lord wouldn't let me. And He's right; it's more personal, more real, to know the author's name and a little of their life, and doesn't have to distract from the meaning of the poems. So, as He led, here it is.

I grew up in the San Gabriel foothills of beautiful Altadena, California, with wonderful parents, four brothers, and one sister. Last year the Lord brought us to a 48-acre farm in Fruitvale, Idaho—a complete change in scenery and lifestyle that we praise Him for each day, though I haven't lost my love for California or my thanks to the Lord for His goodness there. Wherever He is is *home*, and how I praise Him for giving us such a beautiful temporary home here. Most of the photographs in this book were taken on or near our farm.

Living with the Lord, reading His word, and walking with His people are my greatest joys, and He fills my days with writing, studying, harp playing, housecleaning, and farm work—even weeding is a pleasure in

such a lovely place, and almost anything is a pleasure done with Him.

I am not special at all; I am horribly lazy, proud, and selfish to a terrifying degree, and have no explanation for the Lord's grace and love for me. Anything good in me is absolutely Him, and how I praise Him for my weakness—"that the excellency of the power may be of God, and not of us." He is so good!

Please pray that I may walk worthy of my Lord, as I pray that each of you may find the full assurance of faith in Jesus, the Son of God, who died for us and rose again. "Christ in us, the hope of glory..." May He have all the glory and praise forever.

www.ingramcontent.com/pod-product-compliance
Lightning Source LLC
Chambersburg PA
CBHW040328300426
44113CB00020B/2687